Grafted Tree

Family Poems

Grafted Tree

Family Poems

by

Judith Prest

© 2023 Judith Prest. All rights reserved.
This material may not be reproduced in any form, published,
reprinted, recorded, performed, broadcast,
rewritten or redistributed without
the explicit permission of Judith Prest.
All such actions are strictly prohibited by law.

Cover image "Tree Photo" by Judith Prest
Images of John Prest and Jake Chamberlain from family photos
Author photo by Ashley Holley, Wolf Mountain Productions
Cover design by Shay Culligan

ISBN: 978-1-63980-380-4

Kelsay Books
502 South 1040 East, A-119
American Fork, Utah 84003
Kelsaybooks.com

Huge gratitude to my editor,
Christine Graf.

I offer the poems in *Grafted Tree*
to honor the complexity of family
and the diverse ways family connections
have manifested in my life.

Acknowledgments

Thank you to the following publications, where versions of these poems previously appeared:

Geography of Loss: "Father," "Wardrobe Alchemy," "Snake Bite Kit," "Longing"

Late Day Light: "You Are Here" (earlier version), "Borders," "Praise Song" (earlier version), "Immigration Clinic"

Rearing in the Rearview: "An Old Story," "Father," "Wardrobe Alchemy," "Snake Bite Kit," "For Jon"

Up the River: "Wardrobe Alchemy"

Contents

You Are Here	13
An Old Story	15
Father	16
Snake Bite Kit	17
Wardrobe Alchemy	18
Wired to Explode	19
In the Aftermath of Knowing	21
Unsolved	22
Guadalajara 1989: Falling in Love	23
Immigration Clinic, Juarez, December 1989	25
For Jon	27
Invisible Borders	28
Blessing for Jon	29
The Dad	30
June 2, 2020	31
Amulets Against Oblivion	32
Weight	33
Undersong	34
Where Love Goes	35
Territories	36
Praise Song to My Roots	38
My Mother as the Farm in Delaware	39
For Jake	40
If Only	42
Longing	43

You Are Here

Wherever I go
I bring a crowd along:
old lovers with their lies and promises,
my grandmother with her straight back
and harsh judgement;
my mother, who carried
a knot in her heart,
all the girls and women I have
ever been . . .

It's exhausting,
seven decades of travel
with an entourage
of dead ancestors

whose magnetism
aligns the particles
of my dreams and desires:
Great Aunt Carrie, bipolar vaudeville star,
Dad's Uncle Theo, sea captain,
lead miners from Yorkshire,
French Huguenots,
Great Grandpa Theodore
drinking up his pay
from the clay mines before
Saint Ellen my great grandma
can buy food.

And the now visible ancestors,
skeletons pulled
from the closet of family secrets:
the wild pilot, the grandmother I resemble,

living brothers, some of whom
won't speak to me,
who interrupt my sleep
with unanswerable questions.

This explains
my difficulty
preparing for travel:
my baggage is full
before I pack the first
pair of socks.

An Old Story

The story my DNA reveals
slips through the knothole
from the broken branch
of my mother's death.

I am born in August 1951
to John and Grace,
but the father is someone else.

A common human saga
new to me
with edges that cut deep,
split my family tree
like a sharp axe.
I am splintered.

The story my mother carried
into silence
is liberated:
a bramble bush,
of thorny energy,
a bumper crop
of questions.

This solves the mystery
of my mother's
secret sadness,
spawns a quest
that spirals
like a burning star
into the night sky.

Father

—for Jake

When I found out
the pilot was my father,
I did a vertical take-off.
Blew right past the wispy green
crowns of white pine,
ripped mist curtains off the mountains,
shot straight through thunderheads,
into clear blue.

Truth blew a hole in my history.
Lightning split
my family tree in two.
I sat dazed on damp earth,
picked through bark fragments
slivered wood.

Everything changed,
and nothing did.
I see them both
on the other side:
the gentle man who raised me, John;
the fighter pilot, Jake;
who buzzed our lives
in a P47 Thunderbolt.

It took sixty-six years
for the sonic boom to reach me.

Snake Bite Kit

—for John Prest

after my father died
I found a scarlet metal box
nestled in his drawer
surrounded by plain white socks

gauze, a razor blade
to cut the X in the skin,
a rubber cup
to suck out the poison

my father was an Eagle scout,
a gentle man, grounded like an oak,
who showed me
how to hold a snake.

what I mean by gentle is his voice
when he read me to sleep,
I never heard him raise it in anger,
though he did tell me
he had to knock a man down once
I forget why.

Dad knew this: *be prepared*
know how to hold a snake
close behind the head;
keep a snake bite kit in your sock drawer
in case it turns and bites you.

I felt safe
around my father because
he could hold me, a snake
or whatever life sent him
in his large steady hands.

Wardrobe Alchemy

—for Grace Prest

Her dress is bold, dandelion yellow,
bodice dotted with black,
the skirt swirls from hips to calves,
flows as she steps
from the trolley to the street,
into the bank, and out to lunch.

Silky folds slither along the sidewalk,
slide through subway turnstiles,
leafy splashes of yellow and black sashay
down Broad Street.

She sheds all traces of joyless
duty, slips past
her mother's pointed finger,
predictions of ruin and calamity—she
will dance, smoke, play cards,
drink beer in speakeasies—temperance,
corsets, constraints be damned.

In her yellow and black dress
she'll stride across borders, over
the edge of her known world,
breaking trail for me.

Wired to Explode

—after a first line by Morgan Parker

I'm hiding secrets and weapons in there.
This poem is an IED.
This poem will shower the reader with torn bits of history:
The shoes my Great Aunt Carrie wore holes in
from her endless manic walks.
My grandfather's tin lunch pail
spills stale bread smeared with lard.
The coins my mother stole and hid
in her socks to buy candy.

One light touch and the whole thing will fly to pieces, scatter
fragments of passed down memory.
My father in Jenkintown, shooting hoops
in the barn with his buddies,
the Seltzer brothers,
before The War erased them.
The red bandana in Daddy's pocket, used
to wipe his sweaty face when he gardened,
steady as a redwood
until emphysema took him down.
My mother in the kitchen filling canning jars
with blanched string beans and corn,
tasting regret, remembering
her lost love.

This poem is full of trip wires—one step
in any direction will release video clips:
The field of kudzu where
I made tunnels through leafy vines,
picked the purple flowers that smelled
like NeHi Grape Soda,
my first five years idyllic.

I'm six years old at recess, alone, bewildered,
wish I could break my leg
so I wouldn't have to go to school
I climb between two tank cars
at the bottom of the lane,
so I won't miss the school bus.

The drunk and disorderly teenager I am,
desperate to be seen,
stumbling through life,
an easy target, a sapling
nearly felled more than once.

In the Aftermath of Knowing

Revelation rolls back the shadow
that darkened my family,
illuminates the secret grief
my mother carried.

In the aftermath
of this knowing,
my beloved father,
who raised me,
remains my father,
while I, a middle child
become sister to four brothers,
aunt to six adult children.

Revelation arrived
decades after
the lead players
left the stage.
I stand here,
under relentless lights,
hold a cauldron
of burning questions.

Unsolved

> —*after Rilke: "Be patient toward all that is unsolved your heart and try to love the questions themselves like locked rooms and like books that are now written in a very foreign language. . . ."*

What sits unsolved
in my marrow,
steals my sleep,
wrestles me into chairs,
onto the couch
where I sit,
and stare into the void.

If the point is
to live everything,
why is the room with answers
chained shut?
Who has the key?
What frightens me
about not having answers
is that I sit frozen
while my life
ticks past second
by second.

Tides shift, the moon
waxes and wanes,
in the forest, trees bud,
leaves sprout, turn red,
let go after frost,
and still I
do not live or love
the questions.

Guadalajara 1989: Falling in Love

He was lighter than the cat;
Jon in my arms for the first time,
hair the color of pitch, rosebud mouth.
The first parenting moment—
he gets hiccups, what do we do?
He's dressed in a knitted white
baby outfit, like a swaddling cloud.

We wait to be deemed worthy,
tortured with paperwork,
questions, a long trip.

The first days, baby Jon
is dazed, doesn't eat much.
I wonder what he sees,
hears. smells
unfamiliar language—
strangers caring for him.
What does he make of it?

By Week Three, Jon develops
a huge appetite, sucks down
the Enfamil so ferociously
we call him "Milkenstein."
He smiles, laughs.
His cheeks fill out.

I wake several times
every night,
put my ear down,
listen for his breath,
while I hold my mine.

We sit and hold Jon.
Time slackens as we wait
for court, social workers, translators,
the almighty clerks
of immigration.

This baby did not
grow in me,
he grew in my heart
while we sat, held him,
fell in love with our baby boy.

Immigration Clinic, Juarez, December 1989

—with gratitude to Stanley Kunitz for the first line

If the water were clear enough,
I would scrub this worn
grimy floor, cleanse
the dust and sweat,
tears and blood from so many
desperate journeys. I would make
this gritty tile shine.

If the water were clear enough,
I would wash away the
stink of fear, the sludge
of despair. Here I wait
at the portal to my
own land; Here where I
bring my newly adopted son
to be checked, certified,
stamped through this squat
concrete building in the flats
south of the Rio Grande;
here where the almighty
clerks of immigration
sent us; here where I must
lay my baby down on this filthy
bathroom floor to change his diaper.

If the water were clear enough
I would drink it in communion
in tribute
to the others—the *madres,*
the *abuelitas,*

the other babies
who passed through
this dismal check point,
squeaking through
on prayer and hope.

If the water were clear enough,
I would lift my glass and
toast the ones who came before
and after, with no guarantee,
waiting to cross the border.
I'd welcome them in an embrace.

For Jon

—with thanks to Edward Hirsch for the first line

I wish I could paint you
on the August beach, your skin
the color of whole almonds
your hands
scrabble through watery sand
dig hard to catch a surf clam,
your long brown feet
running into the spent waves
over and over

I want to recapture this day
hold it high above time's tide line
step into that salty, wave-tumbled
sun struck afternoon
sit with you on the sand
where waves stop,
make dribble castles,
splash in the shallows

I watch you charge after seagulls
every cell engaged in the chase
I am deaf to the whistle
of time's freight train
hurtling us both into
the rest of our lives

I wish I could paint you
four years old
on the August beach
exactly as I see you
in the eye of my heart

Invisible Borders

—for Jon

I have landed with no passport,
a mother
in the land of adolescence,
was certain I had
the documents
for unrestricted entry.

I stand in colorless
airport corridors,
signs in an alphabet
I never learned,

the phrase book
in my backpack worn,
yellowed,
pages missing,
after three decades,
the dialect has changed.

I see Jon striding ahead
on the other side
of the turnstile.
Soon he'll round the corner
out of sight.

I can't follow,
can only wave
from a distance,
tears spilling,

can only pray
he has all he needs
to survive this
this stage of his journey.

Blessing for Jon

May the buoyancy
of your spirit
carry you over the rocks
without bruises.

May you find
among all tones
and melodies
the one call meant for you,
the one written deep
in your soul.

May you find
that perfect note,
hold it,
let it carry you through
the narrow places, far beyond
ideas of where you fit
or don't.

May you hear
that clear song,
allow it
to lead you home.

The Dad

—for Alan

We were novices when Jon
came to us.
Alan dove deep
into parenthood beside me,
shared endless rounds
of bottles and diapers.

He shared the desperate efforts
to decode what this cry
or that one meant.
Is the baby hungry, or wet;
colicky, tired, scared?
And the "he's sleeping too long,
is he still breathing?"

Alan built snow forts
for Jon, taught him
how to float on the pond,
how to ride a bike
and dive under waves in the ocean.

Jon, grown now,
helps us build a frame
to net the blueberry patch,
grocery shops for us
in the depths of the pandemic,
calls his dad with garden news
and questions about tree planting.

Alan, a hickory, hardest of woods,
and Jon, a thorny locust,
rooted in the same earth,
are teachers for each other.

June 2, 2020

Today, when there's a weasel
in the attic, a madman in the White House,
pandemic in full flare,
fire and murder in the streets,

I want to lie down
next to the rabbit
and the fawn, draw strength
and solace from trees.

When the song of the wood thrush
and scent of honeysuckle
fill the evening air,
I'll find respite.

When corporate greed, racism
and "color blind" privilege
taint the atmosphere,
no one can breathe.

Today my brown skinned son
comes to help us clear our garden,
leaves an island of weeds
to protect a bird's nest.

Today, my gentle artist son
drives from the garden
to the gun store,
driven to purchase a weapon
to protect his dear ones.

I want to break
my teeth on rocks,
fill my ears with sand
and throw my broken
heart into the flames.

Amulets Against Oblivion

It is a dangerous thing to forget
the land I grew from.
Dangerous to forget
frogs and fireflies.

My feet take root
in loam and leaf litter
under the ancient beech.
I lie on my back,
watch leaves and sky shapeshift.

Scents of sassafras root
and marsh mud at low tide,
amulets against amnesia.

It is dangerous to dismiss
ancestral secrets and messages,
the cracked plaster
and worn floors,
the blue walls of the room
where I slept.

I will not live in the
forgetting place,
will not disappear.

Weight

sometimes what
we don't say
fills the air
between us
the weight of it
makes it hard for me
to breathe

is it only
those of us
together for decades
who've mastered
the art
of arguing without
ever opening our mouths?

maybe
what we have
to give now
is the texture,
the heaviness
of
silence

Undersong

the space between loon calls
and the mist that rises
when sun hits the lake

the silence
of snow on pines
after the wind stops

lengthening pauses between
breaths as the soul
begins to leave a body

the swell of quiet
after the door slams
in the house of anger

the notes that linger
under the words
after a voice goes silent

the refrain, the sound shadow
that hangs in the air
defines the borders of memory

Where Love Goes

your face turning from mine
after I speak

the tang of lime and garlic
infusing avocado's soft green flesh

my father's hands
holding a chickadee

my mother's voice
the smoke from her cigarette
drifting in from a different room

the land that holds their ashes
growing thick with multiflora rose

Territories

I claim the kitchen cupboards,
the jumbled shelves of spices to the left of the stove;
I do most of the cooking and I refuse
to put them back in alphabetical order.

The drawer in the freezer holding sesame seeds, whole wheat
pastry flour, toasted wheat germ from the food co-op is Alan's.
The ancient waffle maker from the City Mission is his too
because he is the waffle maker and the one
who never eats the flesh of mammals.

The sofa is mine, and the cat's—sometimes it also belongs
to the ghost of the dead black Lab, who's buried
on the path to the pond. I retreat to the couch to consume
cheap fiction when it all becomes too much.

The sheet rock box built between the three-foot timbers
in the ancient barn is his, when
he needs refuge from my flights of fancy, art project explosions,
can't-find-the-car-keys anxiety attacks. The house was built
at his insistence with my inheritance. The mortgage dogs us both.

We claim the wobbly oak table as neutral territory—
for Passover seders, Christmas dinners,
for boggle and scrabble, big talks with our grown son,
for his green tea and my spoon-bending coffee in the mornings.
The table is Switzerland.

Alan's heart is rooted in the asparagus bed,
that curls around slabs of shale
between the roots of white pines.
My heart floats on the pond, hovers over
the boggy ditches loud with peepers.

The land holds each of us tight
like the marriage, re-drawing and erasing as we go,
a tapestry we unravel and re-weave decade after decade.

Praise Song to My Roots

Praise the slow flowing waters
  of Red Lion Creek, home to water bugs,
  salamanders, sand and clay.
Praise the foamy soup of the mid-Atlantic,
    made rich by rivers and bays.
Praise the fireflies, fireworks and fire-places
    of my childhood for all the ways they illuminated
    night, taught me to welcome the dark.

I praise the white pine that held me,
    and the ancient beeches deeply rooted
    blue sky seeping around leaf edges.

I give thanks for the granite knuckles of the Tetons,
    backlit by high altitude sunset,
    for Mt. Rainier, revealed at last in May
    when winter clouds open to clear blue
  and the Adirondack lakes and trails
    that call to me every season.

I praise the grandmothers and their mothers:
  Sarah Frey; Grace Smith, Ellen Arnold,
  Mary Grace Wolfe, Nellie Chamberlain,
  who went before, lighting the way.

Though darkness gathers, I'm held
    by water, light, trees
    and mountains
    as I carry them in memory.

Though darkness gathers, I stitch
    strong threads. They pass
    through my hands
    to the hands of women
    traveling behind.

My Mother as the Farm in Delaware

My mother merges with rich earth
where she coaxed tomato seedlings,
sprouted in the dining room window
into a dense garden-forest
bursting with Big Boys and Yellow Pears.

Roots grow from her feet
tether her to the persimmon grove
where she harvested fruit
made sweet, softened
by first frost.

Her hands become
the long-handled steel spoon
stirring pots of tomatoes,
grapes for juice and jelly,
apple sauce, vegetable soup.

Creek water and berry juice
run in her veins, her voice
fuses with wood thrush and spring peeper.
She grows wings, bursts
into spiral flight with the woodcock.

The land sits fallow now, a tangle
of honeysuckle, kudzu and multiflora rose.
My mother blooms in the daffodils
that open in March, with no one
this side of the veil to see them.

She flits between branches
with cardinal, grazes with deer
at sundown, follows fox
into her den as dark comes.

For Jake

You are mostly mystery to me
living now in old photos,
and bits of memory shared
by your sons, my half-brothers,
I have one memory of you:
you sat at the kitchen table
in Bear. I was maybe 3, and you
were drinking coffee with my mother.
You were large and loud.

I remember the excitement
when you would buzz
our house in that duct-taped plane
you flew for the Fish & Wildlife,
the one you flew UNDER
the Delaware Memorial Bridge
with your buddy Tony.

You were in the air
over Italy, North Africa, Japan
for almost the whole war,
and you *saw* the mushroom cloud
from Nagasaki from your P47.
So handsome in that photo, goggles
pushed up, leather flight jacket
open at the neck, your eyes a little squinty
—can't tell if you had the thousand-yard stare.

After you were grounded
by that stroke in your fifties,
I know you went home to Maine,
got lung cancer and died
at fifty-nine in your mother's house.

My Mother as the Farm in Delaware

My mother merges with rich earth
where she coaxed tomato seedlings,
sprouted in the dining room window
into a dense garden-forest
bursting with Big Boys and Yellow Pears.

Roots grow from her feet
tether her to the persimmon grove
where she harvested fruit
made sweet, softened
by first frost.

Her hands become
the long-handled steel spoon
stirring pots of tomatoes,
grapes for juice and jelly,
apple sauce, vegetable soup.

Creek water and berry juice
run in her veins, her voice
fuses with wood thrush and spring peeper.
She grows wings, bursts
into spiral flight with the woodcock.

The land sits fallow now, a tangle
of honeysuckle, kudzu and multiflora rose.
My mother blooms in the daffodils
that open in March, with no one
this side of the veil to see them.

She flits between branches
with cardinal, grazes with deer
at sundown, follows fox
into her den as dark comes.

For Jake

You are mostly mystery to me
living now in old photos,
and bits of memory shared
by your sons, my half-brothers,
I have one memory of you:
you sat at the kitchen table
in Bear. I was maybe 3, and you
were drinking coffee with my mother.
You were large and loud.

I remember the excitement
when you would buzz
our house in that duct-taped plane
you flew for the Fish & Wildlife,
the one you flew UNDER
the Delaware Memorial Bridge
with your buddy Tony.

You were in the air
over Italy, North Africa, Japan
for almost the whole war,
and you *saw* the mushroom cloud
from Nagasaki from your P47.
So handsome in that photo, goggles
pushed up, leather flight jacket
open at the neck, your eyes a little squinty
—can't tell if you had the thousand-yard stare.

After you were grounded
by that stroke in your fifties,
I know you went home to Maine,
got lung cancer and died
at fifty-nine in your mother's house.

You were a drunk like me.
Did your fighter pilot days
fuel your drinking?
Did you know or did you wonder
if I was your daughter?
Did you know that my mother carried
something heavy her whole life?

You are a bolt of lightning
ripping through my history,
upending my life.
I would give anything to
sit with you over coffee
in my kitchen now.

If Only

If only time could   become liquid,
future would dance with memory.
Lost stories and my father's smile
would live again.

Fluid time would ground
us, awaken sensibilities we can't yet name.
Fluid time would meld
the origins and the healing   of our scars.

When we wake   and when we enter
the place where dreams are born,
boundaries erased,   past spills into now,
into then, a weave of bright ribbons.

I imagine that I hold my son, and see
my mother's face when she first held me.
A complicated web of families unfurls
up and down the generations.

We carry more than blood in our veins.

Longing

My ancestors' prayers
live in my blood.
Each droplet holds
shadows of their fear,
their hope.

My birth is evidence
of love.
My life their leap
into the future.
My body holds
their bid for immortality.

I carry their history;
it has shaped mine.
My breath, my spirit
a bridge where
they stand now.

They wave to me
through the mist.

About the Author

Judith Prest is a poet, photographer, mixed media artist, and creativity coach. She has two publications by Finishing Line Press: *After* (May 2019) and *Geography of Loss* (July 2021). She also has three self-published poetry collections in print. Her poems have been published in *Misfits, Rockvale Review, Mad Poet's Review, Chronogram, Akros Review, The Muse ~An International Journal of Poetry, Earth's Daughters, Up The River, Fredericksburg Literature and Art Review, Upstream, Waxing and Waning,* and in ten anthologies. She is a longtime member of The International Women's Writing Guild, Hudson Valley Writing Guild, Foothills Arts Council and is a poetry partner with Institute for Poetic Medicine.

Judith grew up in Bear, Delaware, and has lived in Jackson, Wyoming; Olympia, Washington; and since the late 1970s, in upstate New York. She is a graduate of The Evergreen State College and SUNY at Albany School of Social Welfare (MSW). She also holds certificates in Expressive Art Therapy and Creativity Coaching from New York Expressive Arts Studio.

A retired school social worker, Judith gives writing and expressive arts workshops in schools, prisons, libraries, retreat centers, retirement communities and addiction treatment programs.

Judith lives in Duanesburg, New York with her husband, Alan Krieger, and three cats.

www.spiritwindstudio.net

www.ingramcontent.com/pod-product-compliance
Lightning Source LLC
Chambersburg PA
CBHW031207160426
43193CB00008B/538